AF236202

Caption Collage

/ˈkapʃ(ə)n ˈkəˈlɑːʒ/

noun

Artful composition of captions into pre-posterous poetry

preposterous poetry

To art to love to soulmates…

Preposterous Poetry
CAPTION COLLAGE

Abstract caption collage detached from photos – recycled into poems.

The captions are detached from my social media account and combined into poetry based on theme or rhyme – think of it as a collage. The captions have been written over the period of 5 years – for me, they were always little works of art! In this book they are no longer descriptions but poems with its own meaning and existence – no longer secondary. The meaning of those newly collided lines is rather preposterous and absurd but the abstractions behind each poem carry vivid realization of a blurry meaning of existence in today´s social media space.

I have always prioritized words, so in the world were words don´t matter, here is a space for them to grow into something more powerful than a caption.

Photos are captions to my wor(l)ds.

P.S. In the process of detachment of the captions from photos, no posts were damaged.

expressing impressions What
about fashion What
about politics What
about time Captions are
art Malls
thoughts, visits
at night Last
day of shopping
rush
in the year
tired of visitors
the sea

the grey is air
the green whites
the sun never sleeps
it is not dead
it is
reborn
again and again
the perfect summary

        of forms
        sightseeing
        for the sun
without seeing
it's getting late
silently

creative freedom
through the glass
stop for a
moment Don't run
what else to say?
white I stopped
            eating snow Finally

I often ask the sky
for an answer
but it gets dark
and then the day comes
after night

the salt is evaporated
into the sea

some things
are simple but big
some things
are better left untouched
some things
are added over time

                some things are kept
some things
are better unchanged
old chair

we wake up
we fall asleep
so is it some kind
of modern art?
under gravity I fell
under pressure
of my young years
snowflakes often
melt

under the sun

no wall
stands for freedom
not even blue BLOOM
june

though why
to argue about all these
happenings when he could still enjoy
her company every now and then –
simply – by looking at
the wall, as she was

an impressionist 's work of art
made from lilies and daisies
sometimes mixed with light-green
or violet-yellow
just with the small hole
on the canvas instead
of the heart point

re-written history, how do you
challenge the plot of presence What is history
truth
that motivates us to act to see to value beautiful
does it not come from culture or maybe from loss
of culture or maybe from exaggerated cultural col-
lision you attach yourself to the most authentic one
that does not actually no longer exists, perhaps this
true culture exists only on the staged photographs
with leftovers of brick architecture

I embody the cultural collision and
I bring blue to the Temple Bar
I am yes when all say maybe
linear progression of time
is ruined

no life without light
no art without shadow
I fell in love with nature
 since we met for forever

urban fiction

I fell in love with art
since we met for forever

still alive

asleep, in love
same old story about falling

I was young when we first met

              ART IS BOUND TO RULES
she is me I am her
              TRY
 if art is feminine, she is art
              AN ARTIST
              A CONTEST
living is an art
        RULES DESTROY ART
like everything
else
        AND THEN YOU

dangerous semiology of nature
everyone enjoys the October First
I am picturesque-ing the sublimity
take me back

(Ukrainian) magazines out of date
роль неба в житті дерева –
it just happened,
Ukrainian in my head
I am such a bouquet
of clouds Not flowers
contrast of human
and a plant

just go out and you will see
the picturesque interpretation
of cold
in digital age Can you feel it
I read poetry to the blues –
vase and the blue
this is my last performance
before dawn
you never know Unsteady
I still try to embrace you
nature

paper feels surreal nowadays
the choice of words on paper
compared to the words
I will never say
don't let the talks decide

who we are
    different kinds
        imitation of natural balance
                extraordinary but simple

?

I will be

reconstructed
redesigned
remade

I am

a human living life

I played games
I played roles
" in life" – the play
how do you know

when to stop
instead of steady ground
we go ahead
the love-for-love
tunnel
I woke up like this

before Florence ate me, I was
looking at myself
scenes of French redness
stop Inhale the poison of young
years Open daily
the stone with a flower soul
somewhere where we grow older
we carry our standards our whole lives

do you like mine
literatur und Natur
they always find me
society reappeared in a new apocalyptic structure

before our London date

I turned the water into autumn
colours went to sleep
cultural waters, natural bodies
the reality is seeing
rain is water
but blue is my raincoat
I stick dead nature
to the walls
print outs hang over our lives
as memories
as friends

when style doesn't match, we collide
in front of the progress
she reads books I read people
together we go to contrast the rooftops

the cable
    the cross
        the roads
        it went on and on and on
species distribution
find me find me find my belongings
finally, all my friends gathered at one place
assumptions are made based on difference

gothic scene and a cable
did we realise
any meaning of anything
in the room No But we could
analyse the colors
cathedral in front of
museums Holy Holy
holy The shining I found
there is something
beautiful
in gothic cellars I would take
lots of stairs
but would steps explain
sometimes it's stupid
to exaggerate the simplicity
paralleled square

the doors open in an hour
here is where Hogwarts happens
green light
stairs didn't move At all
we didn't scream, silently we enjoyed the fear
dragonfly in amber
you cannot fall
when people interfere And they always do
the rolling stones They are real

the miraculous present
step back and I'm alive again
precisely late to surrender
is it dust or are we in space
surrealities
        old us
                new age
not the touch but the proximity matters
the games we play

there is great thing

when sun blinds you
the only thing you see is

darkness

the window into self
through the glass
the sound of gray.ness
it is empty and beautiful
it stays so only

without human touch

who   is out there

who   is watching
who   is pulling the strings

not everyone is a Christmas tree

in the end we all live in a forest
constructed by people

they place a lake close to it for the picturesque ef-
fect

how to become one of this Truman's show writers

I would construct picturesque people too

if you translate me into a poem
I am a combination in a way
of old and new if to look back, would you
~~/iambic pentameter/~~

art through a glass
perspective But you see it through
the double glass Is then meaning
doubled too

empty theaters full of fairies
the shadows in the park grow older close to sunset
close to us
another park another beauty
another merchandise on the postmodern natural
market
I go she goes everything goes
silver lines against nature that is culture

      empty trams full of flowers

Irish stones with flower soul
sort of survival in the city

      empty squares of great movies, and the
faces

– got tired pretending
we all study theatre through acting

museums full of paper and paint
a little greendom
survivor of the land

let's repeat let's replay, or Forget
one day, we all become a shadow
I belong to the ornament on the ceiling
of more refreshed colour am I just
I am
a

memory of a flower, divided in two parts by black
and white

transparent image of centuries

that
made me look out of age
compared to the Turkish
architectural backgrounds
'enter at your own risk'

high art
meets triviality
of life, all of which is
temporary, all of which
should be clean
to follow
its high purpose
it wakes me up
it's never quiet
it's obsessing
me

with its noise

just a little photograph on the wall

the difference

between art and life

is one ~~imitates another~~
~~one~~

There is no ~~difference~~

I grew up to be a
flower
to protest wind with
my origins

yes

I also grow
in between
and my hair blows the wind

I eat flowers for breakfast

while walking
I was reading Reeling

I leaned in
staying still
through memories

obedience
and feminine masochism
that has nothing to do
with women Freud in art, me in train
flower power
they are always
on my way Even if
the way is not
the right A way
anyway At least beautiful
the burdens of the sea
train is only a background

it felt like me
in my house,
though too cold
to be mine,
too old
to be of my possession
I was too passionate
so I took a photograph
of me
with these orange backgrounds
and went home
nowadays nature costs

money

the ducks
and their symbolical meaning

of my life We wheel
around all day long
contrast to winter

ruins attract masses
nostalgia, the past
to ruin is our pleasure – e.g. art
to ruin people
is another type of art
you need no stones, no cement, no words
you need to survive
on the stoneground, you need to get out of
no words no flat ground
not seeing one another

ruins attract flowers,
not the ones with blossoms,
just green leaves around
the green-green skin
on the grey-grey ground around
the stonewall around the very old castle
the walk is ruined by the clock
and we go back to another ruins –
the ruins of silence

I lost myself in Ireland

the church was closed
for us – a castle
the moons around us
libraries full of flowers
stones Is what I like about flowers
flowers Is the only thing
I like about stones
venus
in different rotation phases
around Earth Sun rises
sun follows around the cold
my moon is many

they fall and we notice no more

the city in lights
rotates
whispers at nights
moon is not the one

somewhere far behind Some
museums

are closed for visitors The life is a
gallery
We are the

exhibition

libraries

in winter are white from the outside
and black from the inside. It's just a
shadow
on the wall Snow

is a condition Some performances
are better left unfinished

movies

you don't see the chaos I am facing

depict us and we watch
wallpapers   life decorations

the depiction of ourselves in

cinema

people passing by
people in a hurry
people drinking coffee
this is our time

I've lost myself To fishes
I keep walking
to keep swimming

a little island in the middle
of the flower sea
and I am just a lonely
ship passing by

I asked heaven to save
me But it rained
and water washed my hair
colour, and the flowers
got to be yellow and I
was saved by flowers
Donau flow carries spring
and other conditions
I see the sun They are in shadow

in libraries beauty is bound
to pages to bookshelves to walls
on the fields beauty is restricted
by fence
or by human steps
in photographs beauty is subjective
in paintings beauty
is art
oh these flowers
thank you
for opening the doors
in front of me We
never fit into frames

growing up
to make dreams invisible

I was holding you tightly
too tightly to keep alive
from the chaos we're made up
and in chaos we look for our nature

the reality is real and
turns so fast around the clock

the things we most
desire are right in front of us,
though never in focus

I attach even if I was told not to Detach

jumping over
the boundaries we
face other boundaries
in our endless
jumping marathon

art is Full of worlds
but none is like this one:

memories. real life. future. past. destinations
and strawberries
united under surrealistic circumstances
of present

little clouds little shadows
eternal sunshine –
they call it "the end
of tourism"-bay – another
narrative got rewritten
new cultural heritage
will appear in art works
of our century Dangerous
people

HELP! ART IS DYING

I feel Beckman
human
touch I don't know love
into to clouds, into the sounds
into the fields Into the minds
apocalyptic art
beauty of decay –
culture where I come from
now you come
from there too Iconic spring
this year, surreal,
untouched, far-fetched
real? beauty
would be too less
to describe something
so powerful

flower and rain
lower and drops
flower
me. is. a form
of self-power
flower I have a friend
who reminds me
of a poem
who reminds me of I am I am I am
and of a wheelbarrow
and of a chicken
and of a holy holy holy
and of twenty-two cents
and of literature that
means the world to her
the nameless
how else to express
emotional likeness of texts

swiftly moving around sea.sons
— re-w[m]aking memories
by taking pictures.que
days spent
before de[spair]cember ends/begins

the year when we actually have noticed
the seasons go by They noticed me as well
walking in the park One leaf has fallen
an[d]other ones — followed
I've seen many movies but none is like the real
life
if you read the story about Pillowman,
you will know how Beckman I feel tonight
the death of movie culture
the beautiful beauty lays in authenticity and
this was the most authentic house
I've ever seen
free
dom of the recently left
risk area follows me
 to the lockdowned
European squares
the new epic horror show is out
and as all of them,
this one is about the house in a park, or maybe
it's not
or maybe it's a dream-hopping

exploring ways to make
a movie out of my life
exploring movies to make sense
of life, to take scenes of light,
exploring life, exploring with and by,
moving Moos
hiding ourselves behind the end of things
confronting the beginning of nothing
in front of everything
here and now
and maybe a little bit later

tourism got out of fashion so I visit photos:
exercising thinking
this door secretly leads into the past
so I took the photograph and another path

my mother sent me a picture
of my grandmother and cherries

I saw a little squirrel, I saw myself
I thought she is cold
she cries for the summer
though her soul is made of stone
cold stone I found love
to stones touched by wilderness
 in the Rocky Mountains on my way to Ireland
— love trip that I made
— and I am traveling now

in Kyiv — but not wilderness —
cultivated cultural presence is here with its past

last November lunch in Paris,
where the homeless ask nor for baguette neither
for wine,
but for a wine opener, which we obviously didn't
have

         you either

fit into London theatres or you don't, or perhaps
the theatres are so packed that everyone tries to
suit up inside

— and I am in love ever since
 with the stones
in the mountains in Ireland
all the nature is locked up in our imagination
but what do we imagine, it isn't nature, is it?

oh now I remember all those trees
 I climbed so high
but what do I know of those trees
of those cherries today Scenery
of thinking what awaits you ahead
some little women never grow up

someone dreams, others fear
to be free or in prison for life
with ideas that became untrue.
too early to wake up
too late to see Museums
like universities need to be washed,
dirty art as dirty truth should be filtered
and seen clean Only in the leaves of grass
and only on Fridays The mood

a woman hiding behind the curtain at the win-
dow leaning
bored with tiredness smoking a cigarette bought
with the money earned today
 today is another day it goes on and on covered in
smoke
 like any other previous day covered in sheets
washed fresh with Ariel and the woman is like a
mermaid herself mermaid with a cigarette

oily kitchen smelly fish fried in the pan and coffee
of a working man
 a working woman that is never tired of coffee
not on the front door – at the back
hiding drinking sipping watching the clock
hiding back not at the door on a porch on the
floor hiding there
their shame of being tired
ashamed of working too long hours
ashamed of having no visitors of having no
money ashamed of having coffee not at the front
like they used to before when they could afford
the front row shame shame shame coffee shame

the sunny it was not
though not so gloomy weather is cold
in February but still green
I am a cold blue print on the old,
I am the orange difference,
the same old new Orange days
coffee, house, love.
wait, did I write a poem about flat white
love is orange
like a poem of light and ginger and green and
gray and blue -
and we dance too

traveling far escaping now
I´ve missed to see the ancient
that was right in front of the moment – vanishing
many poems come into my mind
but I cannot write any
under the pressure of my fear to calm down
to stop moving and writing seems like
letting fears
letting poems drag you down
so I keep moving so I stay silent
to the other side

the camera was depressed without filters
the shades of December. On the floor
two boats. Reeling around real Paris
the Danube flow. Over the bridge, birds flying
high
I feel the water, no, I fell! I fill it in
fully grown enjoying rainy days
and flower poems Matching power

we had a rosy glow on our cheeks
to contrast spring, to show off with being alive
some colors look better not mixed
I was blinded by the freshness of the air
 and by Dutch painters
hiding behind this b(r)ush
I keep wondering if she is just a painting
on the wall. When global tourism you have left
then all is left is local,
what difference does tourism make
when everything is global

detectives not always need to solve crimes
but life itself The smoke we inhale defines

how we are seen.
I suit not to houses
but to homes.
some houses don't

even make it to the island.
you understand Gaelic once you see

the horizon where the wind blows
through the Irish Isle

And once you bought a dictionary
in a local second-hand shop, you are native
I see history

that has never even existed In those uncanny
places the true beauty gets appreciated

when I saw him alive, fighting
for freedom surrounded by
the walls of past,
I thought:

how beautiful
what a spectacle surrounds us,
what theatre are we in,
what is my audience,
what is their taste,
do they have any,
would they applause You never know
when the rain comes but you know

 it will stop

the sudden bell ring
 interrupted the heartbeat of a city
– go home, go sleep, close the doors,
– it screamed, it shouted, it yelled

but it was late, I was late,
to see, the sun?
on the other side of the night

so
I pictured light
I pictured life itself This way
I imitate Life

I happened to be a flower

a tree,
the little tree, and the light
that lightens our houses
that are homes
to others
the geo data forces belonging
onto people that are lost
don't want to be industrial
about it but this city
produces summer vibes
so much the technology does to oneself –
and we are the bridge

we feel

     the old

     the ancient

the history

many historians write books about cities
not many citizens know history of the city but
traditional tradition begins traditionally
after the second time is established

a Rose-diet or how to reuse
fallen leaves
can they sleep
Or are they always
awake? second thoughts
feed it to the others.

human touch I don't know love

     some people have dreams
view from my window

     of girls transforming into birds.
is a never-ending spring

WHY ARE BLUE ROSE HALLS EMPTY?

they'll never be together

blossoms of being unseen
blossoms of not being free,
are we not? paying rents buying shorts
 eating out, to go? getting fees
 for visiting parks
 getting tired of not seeing films
 in the dark. Stop don't move
live your life to the fullest
 visit online museum
visit the plant on the sunny side of your balcony
make friends with it let it, the plant,
be your muse don't be amused
that it all slowed down
the spring comes after winter
wind stops the leaves are green
stop and very very slow
pick the blossoms of being

unseen

...It will never end

© 2021 Kate Clem
Herstellung und Verlag:
BoD – Books on Demand, Norderstedt
ISBN: 978-3-7543-3836-0

Kate Clem is a nickname of social media accounts of Kateryna Medvediuk